UNBROKEN DESTINY

Winnie Starks

Virginia Beach, VA

Unbroken Destiny Copyright © 2020 by Winnie Starks.
All Rights Reserved.

All rights reserved, including the right to reproduce this book or portions thereof in any form whatsoever. For information, address:
Goal Standard Publishing
Subsidiary Rights Department
900 Commonwealth Place
Suite 200-1017
Virginia Beach, VA 23464
For information about special discounts for bulk purchases, please contact Goal Standard Publishing Special Sales at 1-833-491-1200 or business@goalstandardpublishing.com
Have a book idea? Contact Goal Standard Publishing Submissions at info@goalstandardpublishing.com

Cover designed by Yahaila Hernandez
Photography Studio 7
Cover Child Model: Yahlani Hernandez

Winnie Starks
Visit my website at www.winniestarks.com

Printed in the United States of America
Library of Congress Number available upon request

First Printing: Dec 2020
Goal Standard Publishing

ISBN (Hardcover) : 978-1-953941-04-6
ISBN (Paperback) : 978-1-953941-05-3
ISBN (E-book) : 978-1-953941-06-0

DEDICATION

Dedicated to my lovely children Gregory and Jenesis. My love for you is endless and unconditional. I will continue to grow for us, so you have better opportunities in the future. Always put God first and your path will be without limit.

CONTENTS

What If I Told You 1

Chapter 1: Fear 4

Chapter 2: Surprise! What You See Is
Not What You Get! 14

Chapter 3: Rearview Mirror 26

Chapter 4: I Have No Idea Where I'm Going 36

Chapter 5: Gold In The Garbage 46

Chapter 6: You Attract Who/What You Are........... 56

Chapter 7: The Lies We Tell Ourselves 74

Chapter 8: The Art Of Forgiveness 84

Chapter 9: 300 Little Things 94

Chapter 10: You Do Not Have To
Save The World Yet... 100

About The Author 106

WHAT IF I TOLD YOU

What if I told you!

What if I told you I really don't know how to love?

What if I told you I had been touched since I was 4 so I'm really unsure

What if I told you I'm so broken so it makes me impure?

What if I told you my unspoken truth?

What if I told you I hold on to you so my heart can feel even if it's not real?

What if I told you most of the time, I feel blue because everything I thought turned out to be untrue

What if I told you I'm so toxic and I really don't know what to do?

What if I told you my brokenness is the reason for my openness with you?

What if I told you?

What if I told you I don't express to you because I'm scared of you?

What if I told you my heart not with the trend and most of the time, I feel lost within

what if I expressed to you my gratitude for the things, I learn from you that I normally wouldn't do?

What if I told you?

Would you still love me?

—Winnie Starks

DON'T BE OUT HERE BREAKING YOUR DESTINY. HAVE POWER OVER FEAR. SHOWING UP CAN BE HARD. SHOW UP ANYWAY!

-Winnie Starks

Chapter 1:

FEAR

Fear binds you, changes you, and steals you from yourself indefinitely—way longer than you could imagine. You may wonder, "*Am I GOOD enough? Is this possible in my future?*" The cold hard truth is that anything that is **supposed** to be **will** be. We must not fear a change in our now nor fear the unknown. Don't fear asking for help. Often, people go through the most miserable times alone when they do not have to. They could have opened their mouth and let those three words of humility slip from their lips: "*Please help me.*" You will be surprised how far those words take you. These words have helped people achieve extraordinary success that eventually led them to public office and possibly The White House. Sometimes we get so wrapped up in ourselves that we lose touch due to the fear of hurting someone we love dearly. ***Dear friend, don't let this be you.***

I challenge you today to get up, dust yourself off, and keep pressing forward, pushing past the fear that has held you captive. Press past any obstacles and the strength of the Lord will renew you to continue your journey!

My Story

I was born into dysfunction and it followed me daily. Dysfunction controlled every aspect of my day-to-day and I couldn't escape it no matter how hard I tried. Whenever I thought I had an opportunity to breathe, I was slapped with dysfunction all over again. I often asked myself if I'd ever get a break… ***"Isn't this enough? Why did my life begin this way? When is enough enough?"***

My mom "married" her childhood sweetheart. It was a common law marriage, but they were inseparable. Most days, he was her protector and she never wanted for anything other than to be his one and only; however, if she wanted to continue their relationship, she had to accept a few things. She had to accept his drinking, his abuse, and his other side. The other side kept him surrounded by the company of other women. Yeah, my dad was a real ladies' man—both a pimp and my dad. How many young girls or young boys would admit something like with a straight face? What was strange about the situation was that my mom knew some of these women! She even found out about one child he fathered by seeing the child at the school she worked in. She told me once that she said, "***That baby look just like...***" Uh-huh. You can fill in the rest. Now ain't that something! I could only imagine how she must have felt.

That is how my life of dysfunction began.

Confusion became part of my destiny long before I was born. It was something that my parents helped to shape. How is this possible? Can someone *explain* dysfunction?

Despite everything, my mom was my dads' main love. She was never in the streets turning tricks like the other women. In the forefront, they had the American Dream—the nice house and two boys. My mom worked as a teacher's assistant and my dad was a true Jack of all Trades. You name it, he could do it, but his primary job was being a mechanic.

But that was the forefront...not reality.

In the dark, there was true **HELL**! I guess that was the tradeoff—his love was not necessarily a good thing. My dad was extremely abusive to my mom. Once while my middle brother was out at the mechanics' shop with dad, he went next door to get a soda from the soda machine and the machine fell on him.

This was a tragic start to the change in our family life.

At the age of six, my brother had to have brain surgery and learn to walk and talk all over again. They said that my brother would not do any of those things ever again…he did…***BUT GOD***!!!

During my brother's recovery, my dad was up to his old ways with women in the street. My mom stayed strong and did well to keep the family together through it all. Three years after this, my parents found out that I was coming. Both were so happy! They often say that I was their love child—a new and fresh start. I never got to experience happiness because my mom packed us up and left when I was only a year old.

She found the courage to leave the situation because

she knew she couldn't live that way forever. She could no longer endure my father's abuse, which had gotten worse because he drank more. After drinking, he would come home and pick a fight with my mom. Since he was well known by the cops, they wouldn't do much. My father was known to fight the cops when he was drunk, so they tended to avoid the situation when my mother called. I guess they figured that they would work things out amongst themselves.

Most of the time they did ***until they didn't...***

My mother threatened to kill him one day and a neighbor talked some sense into her, reminding her that she had children. It was better to leave him than to stay, so we packed everything up and moved.

We moved from Monroe, Louisiana to Fort Worth, Texas to start our new chapter and our fresh start.

As I tell my story of how it all began, I find my breathing labored because revisiting my past is difficult, but necessary for my growth and wellbeing. I get the fight in me from my mom because she, too, had to fight to remove herself from the life she was living with my dad. I remind myself that she wasn't fighting for her life only, but also my siblings and me.

I've been fighting for my life since the day I was born. I struggled to breathe—every breath I took was vital to my survival. According to my mother's version of the story, I entered the world with my umbilical cord wrapped around my neck.

When I think about struggling to breathe, it reminds me of how I fought for my life and how every breath needs to be preserved for the bigger challenges. The idea of struggling to breathe has followed me throughout various situations in my life…and I am appreciative.

Your Turn: Fear

Winnie Starks

I AM MORE THAN WHAT YOU SEE. I AM BIGGER

\- Winnie Starks

Chapter 2:

SURPRISE! WHAT YOU SEE IS NOT WHAT YOU GET!

People look at you and think you have it all together but usually, you don't or you thought you did—only to realize that you still have a lot of learning to do....

What I have learned on this journey through life is that I had to build an unshakable, relentless, and committed relationship with **GOD**. He will show you who **YOU** are throughout your life. That is the only way to really get it together. You need to embark on a journey of self-discovery with the Lord as your Guide.

It is only then that you will be able to maneuver through life and reach the right people who are destined to be on your path.

You get it all along the way.

You get it in all the lessons from all the victories and mess ups.

You learn as you grow through life.

I challenge you today to be patient with the process and stop trying to figure it out alone! Get with the Creator and let Him show you how to navigate through this life He has given you for His glory.

My Story

My mom felt that family was everything! Our house was the house where all the kids hung out and family would come and go. Some stayed with us until they got on their feet. My mom always said that you had to be there for family no matter what, especially during difficult times.

She was passionate about keeping family together so, when she lost her mom at ten years old, it left a huge void in her life. Her aunt took my mom and her six siblings into her home. Because my mom was the oldest of her siblings, she felt obligated to be the nurturer. Naturally, my mom was used to a big family and went on to have three children of her own and then took in two nephews. So, there I was the *only* girl in a house full of ratchet boys!

I hated being left alone with them because they were mean and they would do stupid things to me like swing me around, causing me to hit my head on the floor, or throw me from the top of the bunk bed. They treated me like one of the boys and I always had a bruise to show for it but couldn't tell exactly where it came from and who caused it.

During that time, my mother worked two jobs to keep a roof over our heads. I always cried when I saw my mom preparing for work, begging her to take me with her and not leave me in the house with those crazy boys. I think my mother felt like I was just spoiled, wanted attention, or wanted to get my way. I do not think it ever crossed her mind that, when she walked out the door, the unspeakable happened. When I heard the door close behind my mom, I immediately began to feel anxious for her return and scared for what was coming.

I knew something would happen and I did everything in my power to stall for more time in hopes that my mom came back sooner than I was expecting, but in the back of my mind, I knew it was still going to happen.

There was nothing I could do to change the situation

or stop the abuse.

My brothers were into playing with their friends, so no one gave a second thought when one of our cousins would always go missing.

Little did anyone know this was the start of my sexual abuse… I was in trouble.

I do not think they suspected anything at all.

The one thing that constantly stood out in my mind were my mother's words that she would kill someone if they touched me. I made it up in my head that I was protecting the family by not saying anything about what happened to me. I didn't want my mother to kill my cousin nor go to jail. At the time, I thought I was protecting my mom and protecting my cousin. My fear helped me keep the secret, but my fear also held me hostage to being molested regularly.

I didn't understand what was happening, I just knew it felt wrong and I remembered my mother saying, "***If anyone touches you, I'm going to kill them***." Her words stuck in my head and I believed what she said.

I couldn't live my life without my mom. I knew I had to protect her and my family, even if it meant sacrificing myself. I loved my family, and I didn't want to be separated from them. I had to keep the secret to save my family! If my secret got out, it could destroy our everything.

I wondered if my mom suspected anything, noticed a change in my behavior, or if she was so tired when she returned home every night that she didn't see me. Her routine was the same every day. I began to be angry at my mom for not being there when I needed her.

"*Why did she have to go to work and leave me alone?*" I also began to question if she loved me because, when she returned home every night, she was so tired that she went straight to bed.

Who could I ask for help without being made to feel like it is all my fault?

It became normal. When my mother left the house for work, the boys would also leave the house right behind her, going to hang out with their friends. One cousin who would stay at the house and, during those times, I would find myself hiding from him and praying that someone else would stay in the house with me or return to prevent him from touching me.

I knew something wasn't right about what was happening to me but who could I tell?

Would they blame me because I kept a secret for so long?

I was four years old at the time and afraid to say anything to anyone about what was happening to me for fear that I'd be blamed—and it would be said it was all my fault.

When my cousin and I were alone in the house, he would touch me in places that you never touch a four-year-old. This would happen often and, although there was never any penetration, it didn't feel right. My gut told me something was wrong with this, but I didn't know what to do. I could only hear my mother's words about going to jail if anyone touched me. So, like any rational four-year-old, I thought, "***I can't lose my mother.***" That would have killed me. I had convinced myself that I was protecting my family with silence. I learned how to keep my first secret when I was four years old. The touching didn't stop until I was nine years old.

The molestation finally stopped...

The weird thing about the abuse is that I began to see it as normal. I couldn't tell anyone, and no one noticed or suspected anything was wrong. It finally stopped when my cousin walked into the room one day and looked at me as I waited for him to molest me. When I didn't move away or act like I didn't want it to happen, he began to look at me strangely, wondering why wasn't I moving away from him?

I asked him what he was waiting for.

"Do you want to do it or not?" My response jolted him into reality and that was the last time he touched me. He probably wondered what was wrong with me because I wasn't rejecting his advances. At that time, I took my power back and decided no one would ever take advantage of me again. It was a wake up call to him, showing him that he was doing something wrong and needed to stop. It was a wake up call for me as I finally realized that I had power too.

The physical abuse stopped but mentally, I was damaged for life. I walked around cloaked in insecurities that held me captive because of the years of abuse and secrecy.

Your Turn: Surprise!

THE REARVIEW MIRROR IS FOR KNOWING WHAT IS BEHIND YOU WHILE FOCUSING ON WHAT IS AHEAD. STAY FOCUSED.

-Winnie Starks

Chapter 3:

REARVIEW MIRROR

All the things that happened in your past is what builds you for your future. It's okay to remember, but don't dwell on them.

If you dwell on the past, you become stuck!

If you dwell on those moments, you can become lost in those moments.

Yes, this is easier said than done…

Sometimes things are harder to forget and move past; however, all things work together to build us and grow us. So, do not miss your present. The present is a gift. I challenge you today to look forward and only glance back for motivation to accomplish your greatness!

My Story

School was not a happy place for me... It was the place where I felt uncomfortable and out of place. It was as though I didn't belong there at all. I was not smart and learned differently. When I couldn't grasp an idea or concept, I would lash out at the other students or the teacher. I didn't care what I said or whose feelings were hurt in the process. I did not like school, and everyone knew it.

During my high school years, I was suspended several times. I found ways to not be in school. I did things that would get me kicked out of school. I fought all the time and argued with my teachers just to avoid doing any work. This usually caused me to get suspended for a few days. I caused all kinds of confusion just to get suspended--that's what I wanted to happen so I didn't have to go to school nor do that stupid work that I couldn't understand. To do well in school, I needed one on one attention and, when that attention wasn't there, I would misbehave to get out of doing my work.

I had an undiagnosed learning disability caused by a lack of oxygen at the time of my birth. This caused me to feel slow or dumb. Most of the time, I hid behind my bad behavior, which caused teachers to not want to help me at all. When I think back, I couldn't blame the teachers because I wouldn't help me either! I had a bad attitude and was rude. I realized that I was trying to hide my disability because I didn't want the other students making fun of me. If I kept everyone focused on my bad behavior, they wouldn't notice my disability.

I don't have many fond memories of school because of my learning disability. I was more of a hands-on person and learned best when I was shown how to do something versus being told how to do something. I found it hard to focus and often found myself tuning everything out or being spaced out. My body was in school, but my spirit was outside walking around daydreaming.

Because I spent a lot of time out of school due to

suspensions, I fell further behind—so far behind that I had to attend an alternative school my eleventh grade year to graduate on time. During my time there, I learned a few things about myself.

I wasn't dumb, bad, or alone like I thought I was. Most students had an idea about what they wanted to do after high school, but not me. I was just glad to get my diploma in my hand and be done with school. I don't recall having ambitions or goals like the other students. I'd been working since I was fourteen years old. Those ambitions didn't come until I was in my thirties. I was good at encouraging others, but I couldn't encourage myself. I had no thoughts of what I wanted to be as an adult. I was that person who was fine with not having big dreams.

After high school, I started to notice a few things about myself. I liked helping others and excelled at it. From the time I was fourteen years old, I had managed to master customer service. I had worked as a waitress, in banking, in retail, and also in customer relations for a major luxury brand. I've excelled at every job that I've had because the fundamental goal of these jobs was to help people. I had discounted my practical and technical knowledge this entire time. I thought that I only needed core skills to find success and I was wrong! Success is so much more! I often look back in my rearview mirror to see how far GOD has truly brought me and how He revealed life lessons along the way.

These lessons are a part of my motivation to do more, be better, and live abundantly. We may see things one way because of the life we have been dealt and the way that society teaches us, but you can rest assured that GOD will meet you exactly where you are! He will teach and guide you on your path in the way you were designed to learn it.

I spent many years believing that I suffered from a learning disorder and maybe I did. I thought I would be limited in the success that I would be able to achieve. That wasn't true at all! I ultimately learned that I am my own limiting factor, and I shouldn't short myself. I created my own self-fulfilling prophecy. It's not always what you know. It is also who you know. So, do you know Jesus?

Your Turn: Rearview Mirror

Unbroken Destiny

Winnie Starks

NEVER A VICTIM. ALWAYS AN OVERCOMER.

-Winnie Starks

Chapter 4:

I HAVE NO IDEA WHERE I'M GOING

There have been days when I'd get weary or would want to give up. I wanted to stay in a comfortable place; however, something deep inside would not allow me to do that.

Your future may very well seem unclear and that is okay. Remember, our destinies are not our own. The path God takes us on may seem uncomfortable; however, He knows what is best for us! In the end, we will reach our heart's desires and ultimately complete the path that He has set before us simultaneously. I challenge you today to release the thoughts you may have planned for your perfect life and open your heart for more of what **GOD** has planned for you! This is done by surrendering to **GOD** by engaging in a personal relationship with him.

My Story

Taking my power back on my own caused me to make all kinds of wrong and crazy decisions in my life. At thirteen, I lost my virginity and started to experiment with recreational drugs like marijuana and then ecstasy later in life.

I choose the wrong people to hang out with and promiscuity reared its ugly head, which sent me spiraling out of control. Like the song says, I was looking for love and family in all the wrong places. During this time, I didn't know what I was going through, but I **DO** know it wasn't good.

I didn't understand how valuable my temple was. Thinking about it now, I'm sure this was a direct result of what happened to me when I was younger. I went through a stint where I slept with a lot of boys because I wanted to, I know that sounds crazy and I rationalized this craziness by saying I wanted to do it because it was something I could control.

However, I also learned that I had a conscience. I was in middle school when I made out with my friend's boyfriend. He told me not to say anything about what happened, but I felt so guilty that I told my friend what happened and apologized. It was crazy because, after confessing and getting that guilt off my chest, my friend didn't believe me because her boyfriend said it never happened.

For the first time in my life, I felt like I had control and freedom over my sexuality. I now know I didn't love myself, my self-esteem was low, and my insecurities were off the charts. I wasn't a hoe, but I was a little fast. Most of the time, after when I had sex with a guy, I didn't like him anymore. Some of these guys were really nice to me—these were the guys that, according to the cliché, you could bring home to mama. Most of them were older and even more mature than me. I don't know what that was about.

In addition to all the crazy, I found myself in a smoking rotation with my brothers. Once I smoked too much and began acting crazy with a friend of mine. My mother noticed that my eyes were red and asked what was going on with me. She was the type of woman who didn't condone that behavior. She was a sole believer that I was a child wholeheartedly until the age of eighteen.

Geez, I couldn't wait to turn eighteen.

I remember trying to leave at 17 once and she made me come home. She was angry with my brothers because she figured they exposed me to that desire. Little did she know, I was already exposed, but no one knew about it. What could she do?

She was angry with my brothers for allowing me to smoke with them. I had become so rebellious that I got my tongue pierced. I hid it for a long time until she noticed it one day while I was talking with her. She tried to make me take it out. I did in front of her but, once her back was turned, I put it right back in. She was furious! She tried to have a heart-to-heart conversation with me about how inappropriate it was to have it at age of fourteen. But that was me and I wanted an outlet and more control of myself and my life. So, as you can tell, I surely didn't know where I was going, but **GOD** had a plan for me. Little did I know that, in the following year, I'd fall into what I thought was love and my whole perspective would change.

Your Turn: No Idea…

Unbroken Destiny

Winnie Starks

I AM GODS BEST SLAYER.

-Winnie Starks

Chapter 5:

GOLD IN THE GARBAGE

The things you find in the dirt of life is unimaginable. I would have never thought that I would find myself dealing with all the tragedies and shortfalls I have experienced. All the lessons I learned through heartache were a blessing in the end.

I had negative thoughts and was unsure of myself. I had low self-esteem, too, but all those things turned out to be the Gold that I needed to find in the garbage.

These things slow you down just enough to appreciate the value of self even more.

These things have allowed me to discover my true worth and have a grateful mindset.

So, I challenge you today to not see every situation as a failure, but rather a push to your destiny-driven life. You may feel that you are not progressing as the world taught you; however, we are not on a journey for someone else. You are on God's appointed and anointed journey for your life. Keep Him first and keep pressing and pushing. You will end where you are supposed to be!

My Story

When I finally got back on track in school, I met the first love of my life. ***He was everything I thought I wanted at the time***—the total opposite of who I was.

He was family-oriented! He had a God-fearing mother and father in the house. I liked everything about him!

He was attentive to my needs and we spent a lot of time together. He was one of the reasons I finished high school and was able to get and keep jobs.

He was a football receiver and very popular. He was popular in his clique and I was popular in my mine. Although he didn't date girls like me and I didn't date guy like him, we made the perfect couple. Perfect match—I am proof that opposites do attract.

He made me money conscious. I got my first car with him and he helped me build a better relationship with my mom.

When I first met him and took him to meet my mom, he said he couldn't date me because he didn't like the way I spoke to my mom. He taught me to know how important it was to have a good, quality, respectful relationship with my mother. He quickly let me know that, to date him, I really had to respect my mom! Of course, I changed that with a quickness because I really wanted to be with this guy. I really liked him.

We had a nine year long on and off relationship and, although it wasn't perfect, we learned a lot from each other. Besides learning to respect my mother, he taught me how to plan and prepare for the future and open a bank account. I built myself up a lot while I with him. I didn't get that anywhere else. So, naturally, I valued our relationship because I always felt like he was looking out for me. But I quickly learned that good things sometimes do come to an end and everything has a season.

Soon, he and I started to grow apart. By my senior year, we were pregnant with twins. WHOA! It was a lot to grasp because not only were we having twins, but we were also still growing up ourselves and living in my mom's house. That was an entirely different story.

Being pregnant was not just new to him, but to me as well. I wanted to spend even more time with him and didn't want him out of my sight for even a moment. There was a lot of stress on both of us and that stress ultimately caused us to lose our twins when I was just five months pregnant.

That really took a big toll on me.

I lost my hair.

I was extremely depressed and this pushed him away because he didn't know how to grieve either. He began to cheat, and the hurtful part was he didn't seem to care whether I knew it or not. It was hard but I had to move on without him.

We broke up until we completed high school, found our way back to one another, and got our first apartment together. We thought that we'd give it another go. During that time, I learned so much. I learned about paying bills, making meals, and being independent. Four years later, we welcomed our son little Greg; however, I still had to learn about self-worth, boundaries, and limitations within a relationship.

I had my mind all made up. He was going to be my forever and that was just fine with me.

He didn't see things that way, though. Being so young with so many responsibilities made it easy to feel like you are missing out on life. When little Greg was five months old, he told me that he wanted to move out, get his own apartment, and experience what life would bring if he was single.

I was devasted.

I had to learn how to financially manage a household alone. I was determined to not go back home and declared that I'd be successful. God was really teaching me that I didn't need anybody—I just needed to increase my faith in Him. We continued to date on and off until I was twenty-five years old.

Then I realized that I needed and wanted more for myself.

I was free to live and be exactly who I wanted to be. I found that Gold in the garbage!

No longer did I need to depend on someone else.

No longer did I need to be with someone to make me happy.

No longer did I have to pretend to be someone that I wasn't.

I have found Gold in garbage—independence and freedom.

I found myself.

I restored my self-worth and esteem…or so I thought.

Your Turn: Gold in the Garbage

KNOW YOUR WORTH SO NO ONE CAN DEVALUE YOU.

-Winnie Starks

Chapter 6:

YOU ATTRACT WHO/WHAT YOU ARE

Understanding the difference between your connections with people and your role in their lives is a key principle. Every person is not meant to be in your life forever. They may be sent for just a reason, a season, or a lifetime. It doesn't matter if it's family, business, love life, career, or your spiritual life.

I've learned that the only way to have these things the right is by having a personal relationship with **GOD**! Let Him show you who to be and how to be in each season of your life. When we are interacting with others in the world, it's easy to believe that what is occurring is about someone else and their ability or inability to deal with things; however, it's really about you and how you perceive things to be evident in your life. So, I challenge you to take look at things from a different perspective and only focus on who you are in each season of your life. Trust the process by doing your part and allowing **GOD** to work out the rest.

My Story

After my relationship ended, I found myself on a quest to find a deeper purpose for my life. Here I was—a twenty-five-year-old single mom. I truly know the struggles attached to that and how hard it can be. From financially supporting myself and a household to raising a young son, a little prince, I did it while living alone.

Soon, I became best friends with a guy named Tick who lived in the same apartment complex. He was the guy who knew everyone. He was fun and exciting and even gave me a new nickname, Big Booty Judy, which became an entirely different persona for me. I learned a lot from the male perspective.

He taught me a lot about self-worth. I can honestly say that, because of him, I learned that I was the true prize in any relationship—not the other way around. Being with him allowed me to express who I thought I really was. During my spree of experimentation, I did a lot of partying and that amplified things.

I had a different persona, name, and look.

I was ready to take on the world…or so I thought. I didn't realize I was losing my way day by day by not being responsible like I once was. I was healing my own wounds by taking a break from reality. This went on for quite some time… until I got tired of living wild and free.

During that time, my home became just like the environment I grew up in. I reverted before I realized it. Lo and behold, I had become everything that I was trying to separate myself from.

It's funny how we come full circle.

I lost my job with the bank. Thank God, I had a great support system and that I didn't sever all ties with my first love. We were still able to co-parent. He really loved his son, and I could tell that, no matter how things turned out with us, he had the mindset that our son came first before anything. That has not changed.

Once all that happened, reality began to set in. I

needed to get my life together and get back on the right track alone. I was living in a two-bedroom apartment and began to pray for a new place where I didn't have to argue with the neighbors because little Greg was always having too much fun upstairs.

God blessed me with a two-bedroom, two-car garage townhome where I even paid less rent than the apartment.

Talk about favor!

Shortly after moving into my new home, I met the second love and of my life. Every fiber of my being tried pulling me away but his pull was so strong that I ignored my pull.

When you meet someone and every bone in your body is saying run in the other direction as fast as you can and don't look back...

All the bells and whistles were going off at the same time but what did I do? I didn't listen at all! I fell headfirst, and it was a crazy ride.

My second love was unstable and the protector in

me wanted to keep him safe and take care of him, but we were not on the same page. He had just gotten out of prison, still wearing the ankle monitor on his leg. I knew better but I was so intrigued by the attention he gave me and our conversations. I knew he wasn't perfect, yet he was tried harder than anyone else to be with me—something that I had never experience before.

I was someone's prize—THIS was what I've always wanted.

He was charming and able to intrigue my mind with great conversation. We talked about our plans all the time. I had all the stability with the home and car, but I just couldn't judge him because I had my own flaws. My son even liked him, and he was very protective and didn't like anybody.

We quickly fell in love and moved in together within three months. His mom and my friend Tick from the apartments warned me that we were moving too fast, saying that we needed to slow down and get to know each other better. I thought that they were just trying to tear us apart. Against our better judgment, we did it anyway.

What do you really expect from two emotionally unstable people in love?

I could not say no because the dude had already gotten my name tattooed across his neck for my twenty-sixth birthday.

The beginning months were great. I thought things were finally coming together.

We got along great. He allowed me to be myself. I didn't feel tied down. I started school to begin a new career in the medical field. I really loved his family, especially his grandma. She had dementia, so she tugged my heart differently.

He was trying to get on his feet, too, by getting work, but naturally, being a felon made it difficult. As we all know, many felons revert to the life they are trying to leave behind because they have difficulty getting work. He was no different. After being let down by not getting the jobs, he reverted, and I still could not judge because I was used to it.

This is the environment I grew up in.

But not to the extent he took it. I wound up being one of those girls getting dropped off at work and school with my guy in my car running the streets while I had to figure a way out to support us all. Later, this became overbearing. I wasn't used to this extremity.

I never thought it would be me.

God really began to manifest Himself deeply into my life even more because I needed Him, and He knew it. My man was hustling, partying, and staying out all night.

That was the beginning of the downfall of our relationship.

We argued all the time and he even wrecked my car—that was one of the final straws because the car was part of my livelihood. This guy popped a curb and busted the airbag out. I drove around like this for a few months.

That is when I realized that I wasn't as ghetto as I thought I was.

People would always ask me what happened to my car and I would get mad all over again.

Eventually, things grew so big…

I remember waking up one Sunday morning and telling him directly that he needed to leave and get out of my house now. When I returned from church, he was gone, and I was grateful. It felt like a relief and I was glad that he was gone.

I didn't know that I was kicking out the father of my unborn child… A few weeks later, I found out that I was pregnant with my second child.

My whole perspective changed.

My mind rushed with the thought of being a single mom of two kids with two baby daddies. That was never my dream. So, against my better judgment, I asked him to come back. He was ecstatic and excited to start fresh and anew. He stopped the excessive partying and staying out for a few weeks. But eventually, he found his back to that life again. He was addicted and attracted to it. I wasn't sure if he could change.

We had a miscarriage when I was nine weeks along...

It felt like Déjà vu, bringing me back to when I lost my twins in the beginning.

It took a toll on me.

I was depressed for a while, but I had to bounce back quickly because my life and son needed direction. I had someone to live for. I couldn't take the back road and sit out for a while.

After thinking about now, I really think that, at that time, God was trying to give me a way of escape, but I was so heartbroken that I didn't take heed. We managed to get pregnant again a month or so later.

I was stuck and there was no escaping this time. We welcomed my second child, Jenesis, and she turned out just perfect. I knew right away that I was blessed because of her. She was my fresh start and new beginning. I knew I had to make some big changes to create the environment that I wanted my children to grow up in.

I wanted them to be a great example of the environment that I had worked so hard to provide for them.

I knew at the hospital that I didn't want to create more of whatever was going on until I fixed what I had, so I decided to tie my tubes before leaving the hospital.

I was okay knowing that I wasn't going to be having any more children out of wedlock, but maybe in the future.

He was upset and hurt but it was my body, and I wasn't going to allow him another opportunity to impregnate me without changing his lifestyle.

When we bought Jenesis home, he was helpful around the house until it was time for indulging in his nightly activities. Having a baby really didn't change him the way that having a baby for the first time tends to change most people. When Jenesis was five months, someone tried to break into our home while I was there by myself with the kids.

The perpetrators threw a big bolder through the window, looking for him. Due to me having a high-risk pregnancy, I wasn't working at the time and had been on bed rest. I was afraid to live in that house any longer, so we moved everyone into his mother's house.

That was one of the most devastating times for me because I'd been self-sufficient and standing on my own two feet since I was seventeen.

Our relationship went downhill from there.

I didn't feel positive about my future and he wound up heading back to jail for a few months and, upon his release, he went back to doing the very things that put him there in the first place. This was really turning out to be a toxic relationship. We broke up and I moved back in with my mom, which is something that I said I'd never do.

God has a way of teaching you to never say never.

Once I moved back in with my mom, I realized that I was dating a man very similar to my father. I was able to reflect on the decisions I'd made and what brought me here in life. It took me almost two years to get back on my feet. My mom was patient until I started letting him come back around again, but I eventually got another apartment.

God told me that if I let this man cross this sanctioned threshold, he would never leave. So, about two months later, he was in trouble and he called me. I ran to his side and just like **GOD** said, he never left. We tried again to make it work. Although his effort increased, it still wasn't enough.

I was mentally and emotionally tired.

I asked him to leave and he refused time after time. I was stuck with him until I decided to remove my name from the lease, forcing us all to move. I let go and tried to move on …

I moved in with my best friend and he ended up in jail again for over a year.

That was my big break…or so I thought.

We ended up getting back together again. I really

loved him. During his time away, I had made some major growth in my life. My relationship with God grew and my desires for a better future increased. I had to release what I thought was loved. As you see, I attracted what I was at the time—broken and insecure without much self-worth.

What are you attracting to you?

Your Turn: Who/What You Attract

Unbroken Destiny

Winnie Starks

PLEASE STOP TRYING ME. I AM STILL A WORK IN PROGRESS

-Winnie Starks

Chapter 7:

THE LIES WE TELL OURSELVES

What lies have you told yourself lately?

I am not good enough...

I'm not a good mother...

I'll never be a wife because of a bad relationship...

I'll ever be a homeowner because you have a LESS than perfect credit score right now...

I don't know what you've told yourself, but one thing that I do know is that, **BAYYBEE**, God always uses the ones who do not feel worthy or deserving to just to show His power! Like it or not, God is with risk-takers and qualifies the unqualified. So, I challenge you to bet on yourself and take the risk. Trust in **GOD**! Proverbs 3:5-6 says, "***Trust in the Lord with all your heart and lean not into your understanding but in all your ways acknowledge him.***"

My Story

After all the lies I told myself, I convinced myself that I had to stay in this toxic relationship.

I convinced myself that I wasn't a good person if I left someone I love.

I convinced myself that things would change if I just hung in there a little longer.

I convinced myself that our love would change him.

I convinced myself that we could make it work and that this was life for me...not anything bigger.

Having a family that was complete exceeded my wildest dreams then. I am SO grateful for my growth.

I finally stopped believing all the lies I was telling myself and walked away from all those toxic relationships that I had in the past, knowing that I was good enough.

I finally walked away from all the toxicity that I bought into my life. It wasn't easy but I know it was truly worth it.

The dreams and visions that God poured into me had now opened my heart and mind big enough to see that none of my pain was just about a relationship.

It was about me identifying my toxic traits and my shortcomings.

God revealing those things to me about myself allowed me to start looking within myself and make the changes I needed to achieve my heart's desires. I knew He didn't give me these visions for comfort, and He didn't allow me to go through these terrible things for myself. From the beginning, He made me realize that He was growing me into what He wanted me to be. I had to endure all those things to be the key for others who had suffered some of those same tragedies and possibly told themselves some of those same lies.

Ladies, I encourage you to get to know yourself first.

Love is not accepting less than.

Love is not allowing someone to degrade you or treat you in a manner that's not uplifting and doesn't allow you to grow.

Love stretches you.

Love challenges you but it doesn't break you. That's not just for the intimate relationships. That's also for family and friends as well. Believe it or not, no matter what or who may come into your life, love begins with self first.

It is impossible to truly give and receive love if you do not first love yourself.

I am mandating that the time and energy that you spend attempting to love a bad situation be spent growing and loving yourself!

When the one who is for you appears, you will be ready for unconditional love just as God intended.

Maybe we are not so different after all….

None of us are different—we are all just on a quest to find our destiny-driven life. Some obstacles are different. Some are easier. Others are harder. What I have come to realize is that we were all put here together.

Whatever is a challenge for me may be easier for you.

We are all here to add value to each other's life and, with that, the blessings of the Lord are released. So, I challenge you to speak your truth and do it boldly in the direction of your dreams, hopes, and aspirations. You just do not know who you may help! In your quest for living your destiny-driven life, you must remember while chasing your destiny, your legacy is not just your close family and friends.

Your legacy is every person you touch.

I demand something different.

Through all your challenges in life, you learn what you want and what you do not want for yourself.

You may have thought you wanted the house with the white picket fence...

You thought you may have wanted the career you are currently in; however, after growing and acquiring wisdom, you realize that's not the true desires of your heart! This will cause you to demand something different!

Sometimes demanding means losing something you may have thought you had to include.

You may be forced to distance yourself from people who you consider to be close family and friends or change that career that you thought you wanted.

At the time when these internal changes occur, you may not understand why. Just know that no two people are on the same path.

So, I challenge you today to demand something different in your life that allows you to grow, allows you to heal which ultimately frees you, and allows you to be the person that you are destined to be.

Your Turn: Lies

Winnie Starks

GO AHEAD!!! BE DESTINY DRIVEN. IT IS EXACTLY WHAT THE DOCTOR ORDERED.

-Winnie Starks

Chapter 8:

THE ART OF FORGIVENESS

No matter what life throws you, forgiveness is the key to unlocking your destiny.

Forgiveness is not for the other person, but for you.

It releases you from the hurts, pains, bitterness, anger, or whatever closes and blocks your heart if held onto. Just remember all things work together for those who love the Lord--the good and bad.

There is no good without the bad and no bad without good.

There is no sunshine without the rain.

I challenge you today to set yourself free by forgiving whatever and whoever may have hurt you in the past so that you may move forward in your destiny.

My Story

Once I decided to put God first, He taught me that it is perfectly okay and necessary to put myself first! After all the broken relationships, friendships, and hardship, I was forced to demand something different for myself and my children.

I was forced to look myself in the mirror. This wasn't easy.

Demanding something different causes you to do things differently. Those circumstances really pushed me to make the decision that I would be victorious on this journey and to keep at it. Those hardships and learning curves gave me the motivation that I needed and did not know until things came full circle.

Naturally, when we are trying to do things that better ourselves, more obstacles tend to present themselves, creating stumbling blocks. But no matter what, I knew that this was it! I could not afford to travel back to where **GOD** had brought me from nor hold on to things that would keep me in bondage.

During this transition, I forgave myself and anyone or anything that I felt hurt me first and foremost!

I had to forgive myself for the poor decisions that I'd made that led to some of the toxicity I brought into my own life.

I had to forgive all the people who I felt wronged me in my life.

I decided to truly take my power back this time with better knowledge and wisdom.

Another change in my transition was to no longer smoke. I wanted a clear mind to discern my landscape. I had smoked for over twenty years, so this was not as easy as just saying no.

I also decided that I was willing to wait for the perfect relationship for me. That is truly hard because I am a nurturer and loving by nature. It had always been my dream to have a complete family where my children could experience a solid foundation, but not at the expense of living a dysfunctional family life.

I'd decided to share my journey with the world. This is especially difficult because it meant talking about some things I never spoke about out loud. Even though I write this heartfelt memoir to you, I express gratitude in knowing that something I have written here will benefit your journey in a positive way. So, you see, demanding something different for yourself will challenge you, but it is also freeing and gets you on the right track for the greatness to come. I believe that I am more equipped to withstand any rain that may come my way because I know that my God is always with me.

Through my challenges, I have learned that my mindset determines my outcome and that my destiny can never be broken because I am rooted in Christ! I don't know what challenges you are facing or decisions that you need to make, but I challenge you to demand something different that will catapult you into your destiny of the unknown.

Many times, we don't know our own heart's desires until we enter a space that forces us to submit to God's will for our life, changing our perspective. If you are reading this, there's a chance that we may or may not have few things in common; however, if not, this chapter should still speak to you.

I encourage you to fully embrace it and just go!

Your Turn: Forgiveness

Unbroken Destiny

Winnie Starks

WHEN GOD GIVES YOU SOMETHING NEW, IT DOES NOT LOOK LIKE ANYTHING YOU'VE SEEN BEFORE. WHAT ARE YOU EXPECTING?

-Winnie Starks

Chapter 9:

300 LITTLE THINGS

> *When God gives you something NEW, it does NOT look like anything you've seen before. What are you expecting?*

I made a list of 300 things that I feel would better my life. Those serve as the desires of my heart. It was like my personal love letter to **GOD**. Even though He already knows, He still insists that we write the vision and make it plan (Habakkuk 2:2). So, I challenge you today to push yourself and write your personal request to **GOD**. Whether the requests are big or small, and if it's in His will for your life, He will manifest those things.

My Story

One day, my daughter's grandmother watched a motivational video by Steve Harvey. He challenged everyone who was spiritual to take the time out to write their vision with clarity. He said that all successful people do this. So, I decided to take the personal challenge.

Instead of making a traditional and empty New Years' resolution, I wrote my list first of 300 things that I believe to be the true desires of my heart. This was challenging and it took me about twenty full days to complete because I got stuck so many times, thinking that some things were either too big or too small to ask for.

I finally completed it.

I asked for some material things.

I asked for something to be done in my family.

I asked for guidance and wisdom from Him and I also asked for things bigger than I could ever ask for in my life like being a great motivational speaker and traveling across the world.

With all these things that I asked with a sincere heart, I am now watching God check things off the list. Many things have already come to pass in a short time. Take it from me.

I challenge you to take the time and sit down to complete your list and watch God move and manifest modern-day miracles in your life just like He is doing in my life!

I know what you may be thinking.

You are wondering what some of the things were I asked for. Well for starters, I asked to be a homeowner and, within four months of me writing that down on paper, I became a homeowner. I also asked for things like clarity and wisdom.

Please be sure to know exactly what you are asking for because, a lot of times, God does not manifest things in our lives the way we envisioned them.

Your Turn: 300 Little Things

SHIFT YOUR PARADIGM TO SHIFT YOUR LIFE. THE WORLD ONLY RETURNS WHAT YOU GIVE IT. GIVE IT GREATNESS.

-Winnie Starks

Chapter 10:

YOU DO NOT HAVE TO SAVE THE WORLD YET

This is one of the biggest challenges for us, but what we must realize is that we cannot save anyone unless we first save ourselves. It's like what they teach you on an airplane—*put your mask on first and then assist your neighbor or child*. It is not selfish because, truth is, you cannot pour from an empty cup.

We often rush to aid someone else when we have not yet reached total healing. This presents the possibility of hindering and slowing down both parties' progress. It brings the possibility of blocking your own blessing and someone else's lesson. So, today, I challenge you to fully heal and not pursue any additional baggage.

My Final Thoughts

This is the final chapter of my personal memoir to you. You've read some of the most personal things that have ever happened to me in my life.

Some things I have never verbally expressed in as much detail as I did in this work.

Some things hurt me to the core of even embarrassment.

Some things I struggled with, not knowing how much to say so that I get the point across to you so that you could learn from my lessons.

I expressed all these things to give you insight into where God showed me that I must heal and grow to fulfill His will for my life and manifest the true desires of my heart.

I am sharing these things with the expectation that you, too, will take a magnifying glass to your life and examine where you need repair and heal. I have and big heart and love hard, but God showed me that I am not Him and I cannot save the world nor the people in my world.

I could heal and share my journey and the knowledge that I have obtained to possibly assist you in your decision making.

My prayer for you is that you read this and take the nuggets that are for you and complete the challenges outlined to ultimately grow and heal from the things that have been hindering you from your destiny-driven life.

Go out and Win in Christ and everything else will follow!

Let your Destiny no longer be Broken!

You are never alone and there is nothing too big or small that God can't fix.

Your Turn: Saving the World

Unbroken Destiny

ABOUT THE AUTHOR

Born in Monroe, LA to my father, a pimp, and my mother, his main love, I'm the youngest of three children. I was born into a dysfunctional and abusive relationship. During one of my parents' many altercations, my dad packed my mom, who was almost full term with me, into his pickup truck and drove her toward the dark woods. He told her he was taking her to the woods to kill her. Fearing for her life, she opened the door and jumped out the truck while still in motion. Shortly after this awful experience, my mom went into labor and I was born with the umbilical card wrapped around my neck, choking me. This was the first of many obstacles I've had to overcome.

My mother instilled in me that prayer and having a true relationship with God is necessary. Having knowledge of those two things and implementing them gave me strength. Not only did I believe I could overcome the many battles I faced in my life, I did overcome them.

Now, I'm a motivational speaker, currently traveling around the DFW metroplex, telling my testimony at schools, women's empowerment events, churches or wherever I'm invited to help others. My relationship with God has allowed me to speak my raw and honest truth, while inspiring, encouraging, and motivating men and women to do the same. I like to leave behind a message of "Never a victim but always an overcomer!"

LET YOUR DESTINY BE UNBROKEN!

A Division of BJ Hernandez Books

Have a book idea?

Contact us at:

goalstandardpublishing.com
info@ goalstandardpublishing.com

www.ingramcontent.com/pod-product-compliance
Lightning Source LLC
Chambersburg PA
CBHW051736290426
43673CB00093B/86